Presented To:

_____

From:

_____

Date:

_____

PRICELE$$

STRAIGHT-SHOOTING,
NO-FRILLS
FINANCIAL WISDOM

DAVE RAMSEY

Nashville, Tennessee
www.jcountryman.com

Unless otherwise indicated, all Scripture quotations in this book are from the New King James Version (NKJV®) of the Bible, ©1979, 1980, 1982, 1992, Thomas Nelson, Inc., Publisher.

The New International Version of the Bible (NIV) © 1984 by the International Bible Society. Used by permission of Zondervan Bible Publishers.

Photography: ©Getty Images, Inc., © A'Lelia Bundles/Walker Family Collection/www.madamcjwalker.com [from, On Her Own Ground: The Life and Times of Madam C.J. Walker]. ©Anderson Thomas Design, Inc., ©Photo Disc, ©Advertising Spot Illustrations of the Twenties and Thirties.

J. Countryman® is a trademark of Thomas Nelson, Inc.

Designed by Darren Welch, Anderson Thomas Design, Inc., Nashville, Tennessee
Portions of this text written and revised by Miriam Drennan
Project Editor: Kathy Baker

ISBN: 0-8499-9618-X

Printed and bound in Belgium

Contents

Introduction

Money, or the lack of it, impacts most facets of our lives, but so many of us know so little about it. If you've picked up this book, that's a good start. Now keep on.

This little book is for people who'd never read a ponderous volume on finance and economic theory. I don't blame you; a lot of those books are wonderful cures for insomnia. I yawn just thinking about them.

I call this book *Priceless* for good reason: it contains priceless stuff for a culture that thrives on the price of stuff. I promise there are no spreadsheets or complicated formulas—just easy reading and nice pictures. Dig in and you just might learn something about how to get a life—a fiscally fit, abundant life.

This is common sense information—not dumbed-down, not jargon-driven, and certainly not extreme—written for everyday folks like you, me, students, professionals, and retired grandmothers. I don't wear a visor, pocket protector, or a money-changer's belt. I don't wear a three-piece suit and shout at my broker from a cell phone. I get out every once in a while; I ski, I travel, I eat well. If you saw me on the street, you'd keep walking—because I look, dress, and live just like everyone else—sort of. The difference is that I no longer worry about money. I spend gobs of time with my kids. I can afford the time to have fun and serve others.

You can be this way, too.
But if you want to get a life,
you gotta get weird.

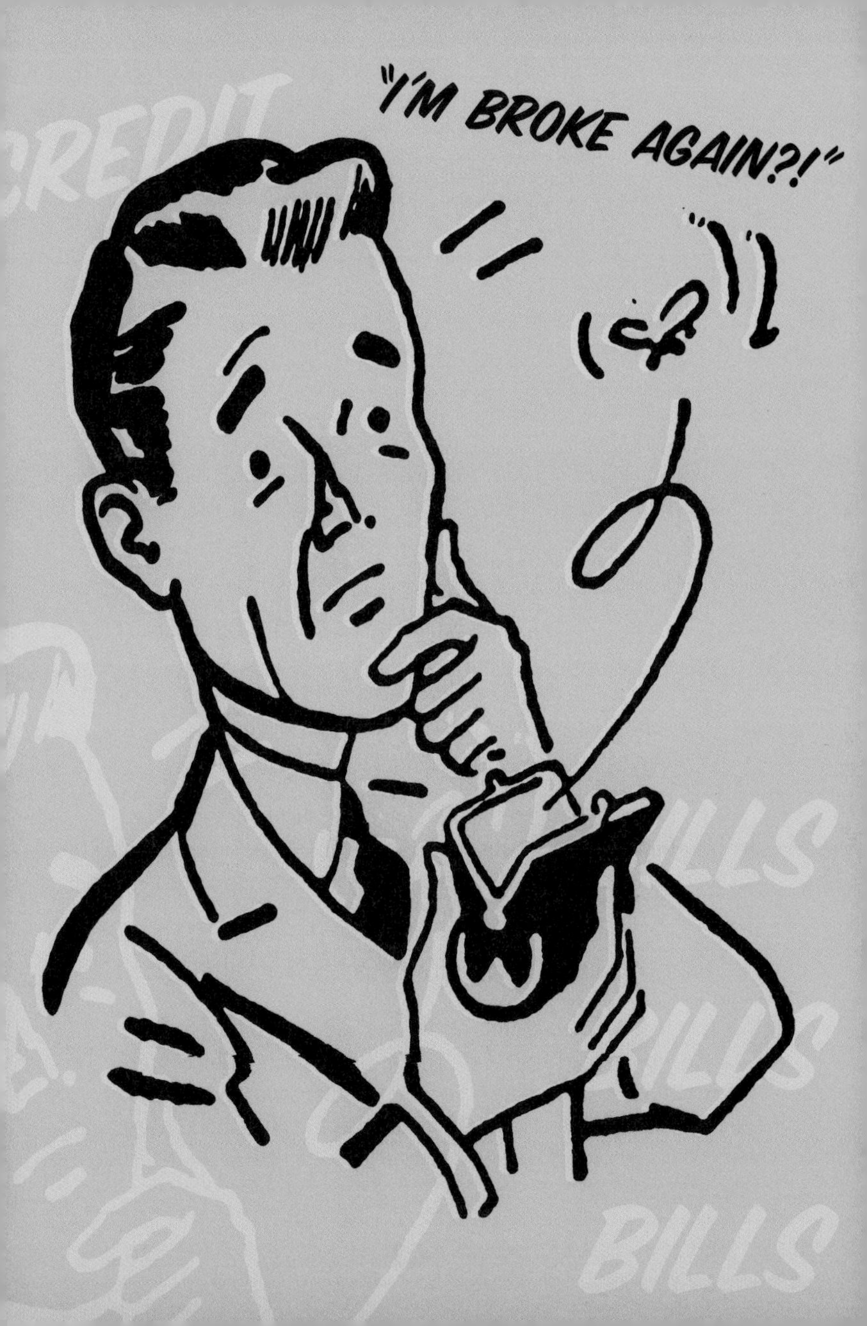
"I'M BROKE AGAIN?!"
BILLS

Growing Up and Getting Weird

"You got yourself into this mess; now get yourself out."

When you were young, did you ever hear that phrase? Most folks still hear it every month when the bills arrive.

My goal, my ministry, my purpose is to make America a weirder place. Now before you start telling me that America is doing that just fine without my help, let me clarify what I mean by weird by first explaining what is normal.

Normal is a relative term; today, if you're "normal," you probably owe on a credit card, gas card, and department store card. You're also normal if you have a car payment, or even a monthly payment on furniture or stereo equipment. If you have a mortgage, there's a possibility that you have a second mortgage, too. As long as you can afford the monthly payment, what's the big deal about paying a little extra in interest, right? You're affording the good life right now.

Normal also has some physical symptoms: headaches; shortness of breath; tightening of or pain in the chest; edginess; disorganization. Some of those same symptoms could be associated with a heart attack, couldn't they? Well, in some cases the two are related.

Folks, it's time to grow up and get weird.

Consider for a moment the concept of weird. Weird is a good thing, whether you're age fifteen or fifty, married or single, male or female. Some people live a lifetime of weirdness; others don't get weird until they're much older and wiser. Weird means no monthly bills on anything except utilities and maybe your mortgage. Yeah, you read right—*maybe* a mortgage.

Maybe not. Maybe that mortgage is paid off.

When you're weird, vacations are bought using money, appliances are bought with money, clothes are bought with money—the old-fashioned kind, the kind of money that is green and has pictures of presidents. Not that plastic thing they tell you is money. Weird is fun without guilt—and without those monthly payments.

When you're weird, you also have money in the bank. You start small—save one thousand dollars, and eventually make another goal of three to six months' living expenses. This will help you feel less stress at your job, which (again) is not normal. If you have three to six months' living expenses, you're not going to fear losing your job as much because there's less at stake to lose. Eventually, you will save for retirement by socking money—again, the old-fashioned kind—into mutual funds, Roth IRAs, company plans, and so forth. Weird is starting to get a better image for itself, isn't it?

Now you tell me, "Dave, there's no way I can convert to weird. I am the most normal person in the world; I am beyond change. Normality is second nature to me." Well, we'll just see about that. If I've kept your attention up to this point, you are not a lost cause.

I should know—my normality once cost me four million dollars. How did I get from being a four-million-dollar normal person to the Crowned Prince of Weird? It wasn't easy; it wasn't always fun; and I swallowed a lot of pride to get here.

I've been in both places, my friend; this side of eternity, there is nothing better than being weird.

How Weird Are You?

Fill in the blank:

On average, I pay ___ bills each month, not including mortgage and utilities.

A. Three, but I count my home entertainment system, new car stereo, computer, cell phone, and cappuccino/espresso machine as utilities.

B. Zero, because I ignore bills. Ignore them, they'll go away.

C. Zero, because I rent an apartment and can get out of admitting the number of bills I have on the technicality of the question. Hah!

D. I really don't want to tell you. Let's just say that I am convinced my bills multiply like bunnies.

E. Five. I just paid off my doctor's bill and am currently working on my department store bill. After that, it's the gas card, credit card, and second mortgage, in that order.

The Sofa Farm is having its big, year-end clearance sale! No payments until 2020! You've thought about a new sofa because the old one has a stain on one cushion and you're tired of the color. What do you do?

A. Figure out that I would get a better deal with the sofa, love seat, chair, and ottoman—and since I have several years to worry about paying for it, I'll look at the bedroom suites, too.

B. How much is the monthly payment?

C. Well, maybe just this once. Financing a sofa isn't the same as charging a meal on a credit card.

D. Go to Wal-Mart and look at slipcovers.

E. Flip the stained cushion over and put back twenty dollars a month; when I've saved about two hundred dollars, I'll start scouring the classifieds for sofas. In the meantime, I'll spend more time jogging in the park so I don't have to look at my ugly sofa.

Earl from the Sav-a-Mart gave you a red-hot stock tip he overheard from one of his regular customers. Earl is usually right about stuff: rain, movie star divorces, and the price of potted meat. He's an honest man. You'd trust him to water your lawn; should you trust his stockmarket savvy?

A. Yes! Does Wall Street take plastic?

B. Yes! How do I call in a stock purchase?

C. Yes! I was going to use the money to pay Ned back (he'd paid part of my cable bill last month), but this might enable me to pay Ned back and pocket a bit of profit, too.

D. Well, I suppose I could . . . but I think I'll take this little bit of extra money and put it into my entertainment fund this month.

E. Actually, I'm working on saving three to six months' living expenses. Think I'll just stick the money into my regular savings account. It's boring, but at least it will stay there.

Complete this sentence: If I lost my job tomorrow, I . . .

A. would be charging groceries the following day.

B. would put my house on the market before the next mortgage payment is due and have a heart attack.

C. would call an attorney. They can't do that to me, can they? Gotta be a loophole somewhere.

D. would be okay for about a month, but I might have to count on raiding my parents' pantry.

E. better be fired for a good reason. But I'd be okay until I found something else.

Finish this thought: My children will inherit . . .

A. a lot of really neat stuff that they will have to pay for.

B. a funeral bill that should be covered by my life insurance, plus a stack of unpaid bills. Wait a minute, do I have life insurance?

C. court fees, 'cause probate ain't cheap and I don't have a will, despite my penchant for loopholes and legalities.

D. a mortgage that's only a few years from being paid off. The better news is that I do have a couple of mutual funds, plus my company pension.

E. my entire estate, including money to pay for their education and/or start-up costs for their adult lives. Since I involved them in the process of straightening out my own finances, my prayer would be that they learned from my mistakes instead of inheriting them. Turn the page to see your score.

SCORING

Very simple. Give yourself one point for every A answer, two points for B, three for C, four for D, and five for E.

5–8   You are as normal as they come. And that's not a compliment. You are in need of a reality check, because this kind of living cannot go on forever—but your bills can. Whether you outlive your debt or not, someone will have to pay, and if it's your children or grandchildren, don't expect to be remembered fondly. There's not one bit of weirdness in you.

9–12   You're fairly normal, but your weirdness has entered your system via fear. You know you're one payment away from the streets, but you don't know what to do. For starters, unlearn your favorite question: How much is the monthly payment? Just strike it from your noggin. Take a deep breath and know that tomorrow will come; you can get through this, but anxiety attacks are not the answer.

13–16   You want to be weird, but you want someone else to pay for it. Now I love a good bargain as much as the next person, and my wife is an expert on negotiating. You, however, want to put the blame on someone and have him pay for your mistakes, including any get-rich-quick scheme you buy into. Your worst obstacle on the path to weirdness is yourself.

17–20   You're semi-weird. This means, you're trying, but you fudge every now and then. You can still be fooled into thinking that certain types of financing are acceptable, even though you won't admit it to me. The good news is, you are making the right decisions three out of four times, but you still have to pay a bit on past mistakes.

21–25   Congratulations! You are 98% full-blooded weird! You've messed up, acknowledged it, and are doing something about it. It's taking a while to get you there, isn't it? But you are going to get there, and if you play your cards right, no one else in your family will have to make the same journey.

Say the weirdness mantra:
Weird is Wonderful, Weird is Worry-Free

Seven Baby Steps to Financial Peace

Step 1
Sock away $1,000 in an emergency fund.
($500, if your income's under $20,000 per year.)

Step 2
Pay off all debt with the "**debt snowball**."
(We'll get to that in a later chapter.)

Step 3
Beef up the emergency fund
with **three to six months' expenses** in savings.

Step 4
Invest 15% of household income into **Roth IRAs**
and **pre-tax retirement plans**.

Step 5
Save for your children's **college fund**.

Step 6
Pay off your home early—yes, we're serious.

Step 7
Build wealth through wise investments,
such as **mutual funds** and **real estate**.

Go to the ant, you sluggard!

Consider her ways and be wise,

which, having no captain, overseer

or ruler provides her supplies in the summer,

and gathers her food in the harvest.

How long will you slumber, O sluggard?

When will you rise from your sleep?

PROVERBS 6:6–9

>Chapter 1
Keeping Your Cash
(Saving)

Start Socking It Away

The first step to financial peace involves saving money; it's a straightforward thing. Saving money must become a priority—you're not gonna save money if you're waiting for that raise, or waiting until you've paid off that debt, or maintaining a "when, when, when" attitude. Once you've had it—really had it—with debt, with stress, with fear, that's when you'll start saving money.

You see, the secret to saving money is about emotion. It's not a mathematical decision; it's a decision to get in attack mode and actually do it. This is a priority-based decision. Waiting to make more money or handing over piles of money to creditors each month is not a good plan for a debt-free life. You'll never get out of debt until you save money. Sound crazy? Being broke is far worse.

Take a baby step by putting one thousand dollars into a regular savings account—not a mutual fund or some stock—to use as an emergency fund. It might take you several months of twenty-dollar and fifty-dollar deposits; you may need to sell some big-ticket items; but that one thousand dollars will offer you a bit of security.

Or another idea for this baby step is to not even put the $1,000 in the bank. The bank might pay you $1.80 per month in interest while charging you a $3.00 service fee. If you keep the money in the underwear drawer you'll eventually pay it to the pizza man. Instead, think about buying a cheap frame to put the money in. Write under the money "In case of emergency break glass," and hang the framed emergency fund behind your coats in the closet.

Whatever way, here's the situation: You've got to decide to start right now.

DID YA KNOW?

. . .that the typical American household saves **2.2%** of their

after-tax income, while the typical Japanese family saves **18.1%**

SOURCE: U.S. DEPARTMENT OF COMMERCE

There are two times in a man's life when he should not speculate:

when he can't afford it, and when he can.

>MARK TWAIN

Almost any man knows how to earn money,

but not one in a million knows how to spend it.

>HENRY DAVID THOREAU

I KNOW IT'S WEIRD AND IT'S REAL DIFFERENT,
BUT WE BELIEVE YOU OUGHT TO
SAVE UP AND PAY FOR THINGS.

- Dave Ramsey

We're better at deciding what we would do with a million dollars
than what we're going to do without it.

> A faithful man will abound with blessings,
> but he who hastens to be rich will not go unpunished.
>
> **PROVERBS 28:20**

A successful person is one who went ahead and did the thing
the rest of us never quite got around to.

It is not whether you get knocked down; it is whether you get up.
>VINCE LOMBARDI

There are no gains without pains.
>BENJAMIN FRANKLIN

How Disney Defeated Debt

Walt Disney remained in debt—heavily in debt—for more than twenty years. After some of his major blockbusters—*Snow White and the Seven Dwarfs, Pinocchio,* and *Bambi*—Walt actually lost money because of the cost of making the films and the extra expenses of operating an elaborate studio. Foreign markets dried up in the wake of Nazi invasions, and Walt didn't realize that simple indecisiveness or change of heart during a film's production costs money. It didn't take long for his company to accrue four-and-a-half million dollars in debt—and an employee union that picketed for higher wages.

Walt pieced together income for his studio by making films for the government, but after World War II, his company was deeply in debt. He opted to diversify the company's interests and created three different angles: movies that "starred" wildlife, led by *Seal Island*; live-action adventures, beginning with *Treasure Island*; and feature-length animated films, starting with *Cinderella*.

While Walt was tightening his belt—including the sale of his Palm Springs vacation home—he continued to borrow: against his life insurance, from his own employees, and from other corporations. During the 1950s, Walt was fortunate to release a few highly successful movies and was finally debt-free by 1961.

It took many years and many films to pull himself out, but Walt managed to do so by age 60.

> **A**nd let them gather all the food of those good years that are coming, and store up grain under the authority of Pharaoh, and let them keep food in the cities. Then that food shall be as a reserve for the land for the seven years of famine which shall be in the land of Egypt, that the land may not perish during the famine.

GENESIS 41:35–36

You cannot bring about prosperity by discouraging thrift.
You cannot establish sound security on borrowed money.
You cannot keep out of trouble by spending more than your income.

>REV. WILLIAM J. H. BOETCKER

First ask yourself: What is the worst that can happen?
Then prepare to accept it. Then proceed to improve on the worst.

>DALE CARNEGIE

Money is a terrible master but an excellent servant.

>P. T. BARNUM

The happiest people don't necessarily have the best of everything.
They just make the best of everything.

I do everything for a reason . . . Most of the time the reason is money.

>SUZY PARKER

By the time you pay all your bills each month,
about the only thing left to spend is a nice, quiet evening at home.

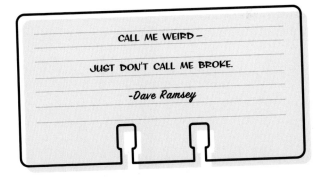

CALL ME WEIRD —

JUST DON'T CALL ME BROKE.

-Dave Ramsey

Savings Tip

If you save **$100 dollars**

each month for forty years

(12% interest), you'll end up with

$1,188,242.

> In the house of the wise are stores of choice food and oil,
> but a foolish man devours all he has.
>
> **PROVERBS 21:20, NIV**

Spare no expense to make everything as economical as possible.

>SAMUEL GOLDWYN

Money is like a reputation for ability—more easily made than kept.

>SAMUEL BUTLER

The safest way to double your money
is to fold it over once and put it in your pocket.

>FRANK MCKINNEY HUBBARD

GRANDMA SAID TO SAVE
FOR UNEXPECTED EVENTS,
DIDN'T SHE?
SHE SAID TO SAVE FOR A RAINY DAY.

-Dave Ramsey

If you can live like no one else will,

then you eventually will live like no one else can.

Money begets money.

>ITALIAN PROVERB

It is better to have a hen tomorrow than an egg today.

Having it all doesn't necessarily mean having it all at once.

>STEPHANIE LUETKEHANS

Anybody can make a fortune.

It takes a genius to hold on to one.

>JAY GOULD (ATTRIBUTED)

Money is flat and meant to be piled up.

>SCOTTISH PROVERB

If riches increase, do not set your heart on them.

PSALMS 62:10

How to Get a "Free" Car

Some people will buy an $18,000 car financed for seven years at 10% payments of $300. After seven years, the car will be worth about $800.

Our option would be to buy a $6,000 car, finance (if necessary) at 10% payments of $100, and save the other $200. After seven years, the car will be worth about $400. Watch what happens next:

At Year Seven:

Savings	$24,190
Purchase last year's car w/cash	16,000
Left in savings*	$ 8,190

*Continue to make "payments" of $300 to your savings account.

After another seven years, look at what happens:

You've saved (at 10% return)	$52,245
Purchase last year's model car w/cash	25,000
Left in savings	$27,245

Continue this purchasing pattern, and you'll never have a car payment again!

Testimonials

"I had about $19,000 in credit card and car debt. I have now paid off the card and owe only $6,400 in debt. It has been slow; I work full-time and I am in the National Guard, too. I am a single parent of two great kids, so I refuse to work any more jobs, but now I have a plan. Thank you! Thank you! Thank you! There is light at the end of the tunnel!" —Stephanie

"We no longer look at ten dollars or twenty dollars—or any other amount—as insignificant. My wife and I have paid off nearly every debt over the past three years (and I can't begin to tell you how that feels)! My father always carried a knife everywhere; it was a great tool and had many uses on the farm where I grew up. But money, like a knife, can be very dangerous if you are not taught first how to use it. Thank you!" —Scott and Robyn

"We had just gotten our $1000 emergency fund in place when our twelve-year-old son had an emergency appendectomy. He had complications and stayed in the hospital a week. After the health insurance paid their share and we got the final bill from the hospital, I took it to the business office at the hospital and asked them if I paid the balance in full could I get a discount. They gave us twenty-five percent off and saved us $225.**" —Tony and Charlotte**

"I wanted to share with you how important the emergency fund was for us. When we were first saving it, we had $174 in it and my husband's car needed work. The bill was $178. Once again we started saving and managed to get $502 in it. Then the refrigerator went out and we bought a used one for $487. Thank goodness for that emergency fund! We now have $1,000 in it and have begun tackling our debt snowball!**" —Peggy**

Chapter 2

How To Eat an Elephant
(Cash Flow Planning)

For which of you,

intending to build a tower,

does not sit down first and count the cost,

whether he has enough to finish it—lest,

after he has laid the foundation,

and is not able to finish,

all who see it begin to mock him, saying,

"This man began to build

and was not able to finish."

LUKE 14:28–30

Budgeting One Bite at a Time

Let's just go ahead and get the ugliness out in the open: prepare a budget. Now you're telling me, "Dave, I don't want to do a budget. A budget means you're going to control me." If you think a budget forbids you to have any fun, you don't have much experience with them.

Any sort of cash flow plan begins with a budget; this stuff will get confusing otherwise. I mean, here we are, talking about retirement planning, college funding, insurance, investments—and we're also talking about getting out of debt. And it's all coming at you, and you're thinking, "I've got to do all of this?!? Where am I supposed to start?" Like I said, start with a budget.

That's how you eat an elephant—one bite at a time. Cramming it in, all at once, practically guarantees that you'll choke.

Back in my big-spending days, Sharon and I decided that the cool thing to do was to take a ski trip to Aspen—never mind that neither of us had set even a toe inside a pair of skis. What we actually bought was an illusion—we flew directly into Aspen, rented the snazzy condo on the slope, got the best ski equipment—and (reality check) discovered that we could actually get hurt out there!

Swallowing a bit of pride, we hopped a bus and traveled a couple of miles away to a place called Buttermilk mountain. To give you an idea, once you've conquered the first slope the instructors put you on, then you graduate to the bunny slope. By the time we arrived at the bunny slope, I felt like I was getting somewhere. (We still had to conquer the chair lift, but that's another story.) Now, over ten years and many slopes later, we're skiing blacks and blues and any other mountainsides we can find. And afford.

This is a process, a journey; it is crucial to walk, not skip, through each step. If you're intent on building a tower, sit down first and make sure you can afford to do so; you don't want to start a particular foundation and discover that there's nothing left over to finish it. Budgeting is a must.

Start by balancing your checkbook, no matter how painful the task. Be forewarned: rubber checks are a sign of crisis living. Get out of that cycle and balance your checkbook. The next step is to abandon your anytime teller card—those things are an invitation to Impulse City. The third step is to (gulp) develop a budget that can account for every dollar that comes into your household, including the dollars allotted for "blowing." Don't overcomplicate the budget, but do include every possible expense that can be forethought. You will not have the same expenses, month-end and month-out, so be prepared to create a new budget each month.

Save yourself, save your marriage, and forget crisis management— get a cash flow plan in place that helps you pay off the past, manage the present, and prepare for the future.

Priorities are reflected in the things we spend money on.

Far from being a dry accounting of bookkeepers,

a nation's budget is full of moral implications;

it tells what a society cares about and what it does not care about;

it tells what its values are.

>J. W. FULBRIGHT

YOU CAN'T DO THIS PERFECT, GENERIC BUDGET—
LIFE IS NOT DIVIDED BY TWELVE.
ONCE YOU'VE CREATED A BUDGET THE FIRST TIME,
IT WON'T TAKE LONG
TO ADJUST IT EACH MONTH
TO MAKE IT REALITY-BASED AND REAL.
-Dave Ramsey

Remember the tea kettle.

Though up to its neck in hot water, it continues to sing.

The plans of the diligent lead surely to plenty,
but those of everyone who is hasty, surely to poverty.

PROVERBS 21:5

Just about the time your income gets to the point
where food prices don't matter—calories do.

Two sisters, living on their own for the fist time, had trouble making
ends meet. One day they were sitting at their kitchen table going
through the bills that had come in the morning's mail. After opening
one envelope, the younger of the two let out a great sigh of relief.
"Good news," she said to her sister. "It looks like they're willing
to forget this bill—it says right here it's their final notice."

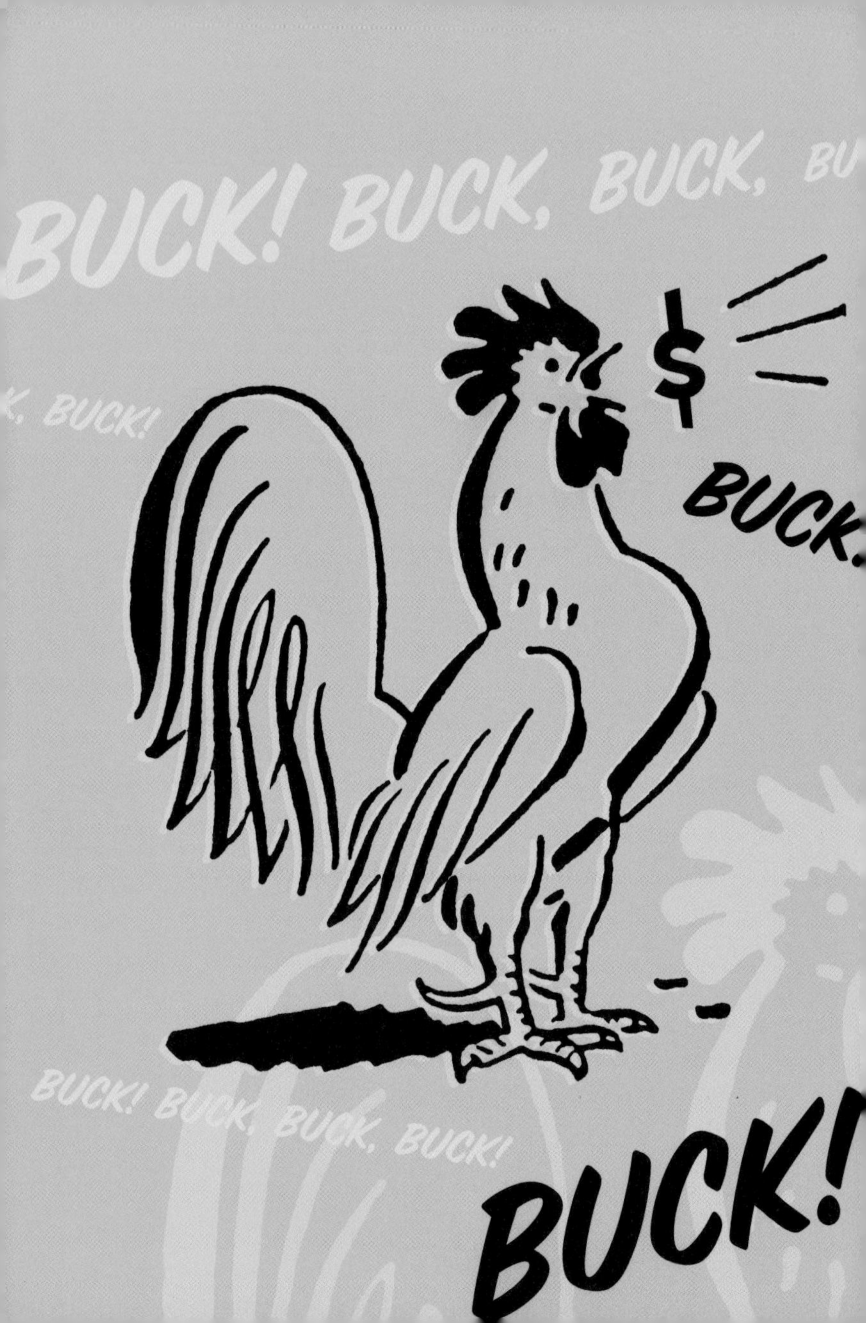
BUCK! BUCK, BUCK,
BUCK!
$
BUCK
BUCK! BUCK, BUCK, BUCK!
BUCK!

It's Never Too Late

"Colonel" Harland Sanders was born in Henryville, Indiana, and lived there until he was about twelve. His father had died when he was about six, and with his mother entering the workforce, Sanders was pretty much given charge of his young siblings—and that included feeding them. By age seven, Sanders could cook several different dishes. His mother eventually remarried, and his new stepfather sent the children away, forcing Sanders to fend for himself.

Over the next twenty-five years, Sanders' jobs ranged from insurance salesman to steamboat operator. Eventually, he was running his own service station and began cooking for hungry travelers, often feeding them at his own dining room table in the living quarters adjacent to the station. Eventually, he'd earned enough money to buy the motel and restaurant across the street—a good thing, because business was booming. It was during these years that he perfected his secret blend of eleven herbs and spices that is still used today. What he didn't count on was an interstate highway that was built to bypass the Kentucky town that housed his business. The Colonel found himself deeply in debt and dried up in the restaurant business.

He auctioned his operations and lived on his meager Social Security checks. Sanders believed in the success of his recipe, however, and decided to try his hand at franchising. Traveling by car, he visited restaurants and cooked chicken for their owners and employees. If enough interest was generated, Sanders and the restaurant owner agreed on a handshake that the restaurant would pay Sanders a nickel per chicken sold. Twelve years later (1964), Sanders had more than six hundred franchises and sold his interest to a group of private investors for two million dollars. Sanders remained the spokesperson for the company until his death in 1980. Although he experienced many setbacks during his "prime" years, Harlan Sanders did what it took to get out of debt and started a company at age 65 with $105 Social Security checks; today, most of us still refer to that company as Kentucky Fried Chicken.

Feeling Your Finances

I love computers. I'm into computers. I believe in computers. But as an experienced money counselor, I'm going to tell you to stay out of them for at least the first thirty to ninety days after organizing a budget and here's why: in ninety-eight percent of households only one spouse enjoys computers. The interaction and relationship issues are paramount to the success of marriages or money. If you're single and want to go ahead and use a computer, fine; but I warn you ahead of time, don't get into playing computer and fail to get your budget straightened out. I suggest sitting down and breaking out the yellow pad and ten-key; there's something about writing it down and working through it by hand that makes you feel it more.

News Flash about Cash

Of 100 People Age 65*:

97 cannot write a check for $600,

54 are still working

3 are financially free.

*SOURCE: USA TODAY

Wherefore art thou, my net dough?

I have used a compilation of several sources and my own experience to derive the suggested percentage guidelines. These are only recommended percentages and will change dramatically if you have a very high or very low income. For instance, if you have a very low income, your necessities percentages will be high. If you have a high income your necessities will be a lower percentage of income and hopefully savings (not debt) will be higher than recommended.

Item	Actual %	Recommended %
Charitable Gifts	_____	10–15
Saving	_____	5–10
Housing	_____	25–35
Utilities	_____	5–10
Food	_____	5–15
Transportation	_____	10–15
Clothing	_____	2–7
Medical/Health	_____	5–10
Personal	_____	5–10
Recreation	_____	5–10
Debts	_____	5–10

Why do people complain about cash-flow problems?
It's really very simple . . . you get some cash and out it flows.

How come when something tickles your fancy
it usually beats up your pocketbook?

Extravagance is the foolish spending of someone else,
whom you wish you could afford to emulate.

WHEN I SAY BALANCING THE CHECKBOOK,
I DON'T MEAN BRINGING THE TOTAL DOWN
THE RIGHT HAND SIDE.
I MEAN RECONCILING IT BACK
WITH THE BANK STATEMENT.
-Dave Ramsey

> LET ME TALK REAL STRAIGHT TO YOU
> IF YOU'RE STRUGGLING WITH YOUR MONEY:
> IF YOU'RE ONE OF THOSE WHO SAYS,
> "I CAN'T DO A BUDGET, I DON'T HAVE ENOUGH
> TO PAY FOR EVERYTHING."
> FRIEND, IF YOU'RE STRUGGLING,
> YOU NEED ONE WORSE THAN ANYBODY.
> —*Dave Ramsey*

A fixed income is what's left over after you've fixed
the washing machine, the TV, the car, and the kid's bike.

A checkbook is a funny thing;
once you've started it, it's hard to put it down until you've finished it.

Thanks to automatic teller machines,
you're always conveniently close to being broke.

A creditor is a person with a better memory than a debtor.

Budgeting is people telling their money where to go
instead of asking where it went.

>JOHN C. MAXWELL

Despite the cost of living, it's still popular.

May He give you the desire of your heart
and make all your plans succeed.

PSALM 20:4, NIV

So what if our forefathers had to haul water from the well?
At least they didn't have to stay up nights
trying to figure out how to pay for the bucket.

When we are young, we try to hide our poverty.
When we grow older, we brag about it.

Everybody wants their ship to come in,
but not many are willing to swim out and tow it to shore.

You can't spend your way out of guilt.

Debt is something you get into
when you spend as much as you claim to earn.

IF YOU GET IN A SITUATION WHERE YOU DON'T KNOW
IF YOU CAN KEEP THE LIGHTS ON
BECAUSE YOU'RE PAYING THE CREDIT CARD COMPANY,
YOU'VE GOT YOUR PRIORITIES OUT OF WHACK.
TAKE CARE OF NECESSITIES FIRST.
-Dave Ramsey

Testimonials

"I wanted to let you know what my wife and I have accomplished during the past thirty-six months. We have been married for twenty-five years, have three grown children, and three grandsons. Over the past twenty-two years we got ourselves into credit card debt to the tune of approximately $91,000. Even though we work [and are] doing pretty well, we constantly bought on credit cards. Nor did we have a budget.

I began to start my own program in 1998; I wanted to have no bills by 2000! Other than our house payment and my wife's payroll deduction, we are debt free and now saving more on our 401(k)s. We have both opened up Roth IRAs and pay tithes and offerings consistently, have an emergency fund, and a monthly budget!"

—Jacksonville, Fla.

"For years I've tried different gimmicks to interest my wife in some kind—any kind—of budgeting. A couple of years ago, my newest idea caused her to head straight for the grocery store and blow up my carefully crafted scheme. We've still got frozen vegetables in the freezer from that silent skirmish. We keep a white-board on the wall of our living room for messages and reminders. Imagine my surprise last November when I walked through the door after work and saw these big, bold words on the whiteboard: "THE PLAN!" Underneath were rows of figures showing balances, interest rates, and payments-to-payoff for all our debts. Debt Snowball and awaaaaay! God bless you, sir."

—Mike

Chapter 3

Relating With Money
(Finance & the Family)

With all lowliness and gentleness,

with long-suffering,

bearing with one another in love,

endeavoring to keep the unity

of the Spirit in the bond of peace.

EPHESIANS 4:2–3

Balanced Accountability

For whatever reason, relationships and money go hand in hand; one affects the other and vice-versa. Whether you're single or married, you need to get them harmonizing or everything will be flat or sharp; that's the truth.

My wife Sharon brings a lot to our company—she is a major reason for The Lampo Group's success. When I look at her and think about her influence on my life, I am reminded of a story I heard about George and Barbara Bush. Apparently, they were on the campaign trail and pulled over for a tank of gas. The attendant happened to be an old high school sweetheart of Barbara's, and George later remarked, "Just think, if you'd married him, you'd be the wife of a gas station attendant." And Barbara's response was, "George, you're confused. If I had married him, he would have been the president of the United States."

Men and women—did you know that they're different? Well, okay, there are the obvious differences, but we actually handle money differently and regard money differently. Most men appear to be task-oriented; they want maximum, tangible results. Women tend to be more security-oriented; they want to know something's there in the bank and it's not going to go away. Now, I'm not talking absolutes here; there are always exceptions. But we interview hundreds of people, and the trends tend to fall under those descriptions.

We also handle shopping differently; women want to hunt, men want to negotiate. Did you know some women can go shopping and not buy anything? They can linger over items, and file the information away for future reference. Men, on the other hand, want to zero in on the target, kill it, and drag it to the car. We want to win or conquer, so to speak.

Lack of money affects us differently, too. Men lose self-esteem when they're beset with financial woes. They feel like failures. Women, on the other hand, respond to money problems with fear; it's a security issue for them. So if fear and low self-esteem are married, can you imagine the explosion that occurs when the bills don't get paid? I can tell you what happens—because Sharon and I were there. This is not some Ramsey airy-fairy philosophy—I lived this stuff, we lived this stuff. And the best part is, Sharon and I survived it.

Ladies, here's your job: if you're facing financial difficulty, you need to polish your husband's armor each morning. I know you're scared, but make sure he knows you believe in him.

Men, here's your job: one million hugs. Bare minimum of five each day. Not sex; just hugs. Reassure her that "we're going to be OK again, and we're in this together." Men, we don't think about winding up living under a bridge; women do. It doesn't occur to us that bridge living is a reality until it actually happens. Women think about it a lot in advance.

Single people have it doubly hard—they have to do everything themselves, including telling the spender side of them that the money's not there to make a certain purchase. I picture those little cartoon devils and angels on their shoulders:

"I deserve this. I think I'll buy it."

"You can't. It's not in the budget."

"But I've had a hard day/week/month."

"And you have an empty bank account. Keep moving."

Of course, it depends on your money perspective as to which lines belong to which cartoon character; spenders will say one thing, tightwads will say another.

Regardless of your marital status, everyone needs to develop a financial accountability relationship with someone, and I don't recommend developing it with your shopping buddy. This relationship is crucial because it keeps you honest. You want the money woes to stop? You want to provide for your family, even after you're gone? You want to teach your children so that they do not have to feel the strain you've felt? Then start relating—with money, with others about money, and with yourself about money.

DID YA KNOW?

. . . that the number one cause of divorce
is financial issues?

Meekness is not weakness; it is power under control.

Better a steady dime than a rare dollar.

>JEWISH SAYING

USE THE TASK ORIENTATION OF MEN
AND THE PROCESS ORIENTATION OF WOMEN
WHEN DOING YOUR PURCHASING—
THEN YOU CAN ENJOY THE WHOLE THING.
—Dave Ramsey

Too many people buy things on the "lay-awake" plan.

Train up a child in the way he should go,
and when he is old he will not depart from it.

PROVERBS 22:6

Our grandparents were too busy earning a living
to read books about how to stop worrying.

The great gift of family life is to be intimately acquainted
with people you might never even introduce yourself to,
had life not done it for you.

>KENDALL HAILEY

Some banking customers treat their withdrawal slips
like take-out menus.

Building Lincoln's Legacy

Abraham Lincoln struggled to educate himself and worked hard at his success. He had a knack for storytelling and was a quick study. After working in various jobs and losing a bid for the Illinois state legislature, Lincoln wound up entering into a business partnership with William Berry and operating his own store. Berry died an untimely death, and Lincoln incurred all outstanding business debts to the tune of about $1,100. Accepting responsibility, Lincoln worked as the town postmaster and eventually deputy surveyor for the New Salem, (Illinois) county to straighten out his finances. Both jobs served him well and enabled him to become debt-free.

The jobs not only helped him financially, however; they helped Lincoln broaden his circle and gain a seat in the Illinois state legislature. From there, he became a lawyer and was elected to the United States Congress. Of course, you know the rest of the story . . . Lincoln remained true to his values and honed his gifts to become one of the most revered presidents in United States history. Lincoln's administration abolished slavery and helped others to understand equality and to value education. Lincoln stands as an example of how paying off a small debt can ultimately benefit an entire society for many generations.

Ways to Encourage Children to Handle Money Properly

Set up a "commission" system rather than an allowance. Determine age-appropriate tasks and pay one dollar for each task completed within a certain period of time. Keep a chart; organize it according to tasks or timeframe (monthly, weekly, daily). A four-year-old may not make a neat bed, for example, but it gets the point across to have him try anyway.

Allow children to participate in the bill-paying process. When our daughter was nine, she filled out the checks. We had to show her what went where, but eventually she understood that money had to be paid for certain things she enjoyed; Mommy and Daddy didn't have fairies and elves magically provide them with electricity and running water.

Use a clear container to keep their commissions in. Children are visual, it helps them to see the money pile up. My son has made a fuzzy connection that by making his bed each morning, it could eventually earn him a G. I. Joe.

If your children are a bit older, put them on an envelope system that categorizes their spending: treats, toys, books, clothing, whatever they would normally want to purchase. This helps teach value judgments, too.

Have your children contribute to their own college funds or debt-free funds.

Encourage your child to tithe.

If your children have saved enough money, take them to the bank to sign up for a savings account and allow them to participate in the process. Make sure the monthly statement is addressed to your child, not just you.

She is clothed in strength and dignity; she can laugh at the days to come. She speaks with wisdom, and faithful instruction is on her tongue. She watches over the affairs of her household and does not eat the bread of idleness.

PROVERBS 31: 25-27, NIV

Men who treat women as helpless and charming playthings deserve women who treat men as delightful and generous bank accounts.

Will power is the ability to make your heirs behave by threatening to cut them out of it.

Money brings some happiness.
But after a certain point it just brings more money.

>NEIL SIMON

Failure is the opportunity to begin again more intelligently.

>HENRY FORD

Money may not be everything,
but it does keep you in touch with your children.

Thousands upon thousands are yearly brought into a state
of real poverty by their great anxiety not to be thought poor.

>WILLIAM COBBETT

WHEN MY DAUGHTER RACHEL WAS IN KINDERGARTEN,
HER TEACHER ASKED HER
WHAT HER DADDY DID FOR A LIVING.
SHE ANSWERED, "HE CUTS UP CREDIT CARDS."
-Dave Ramsey

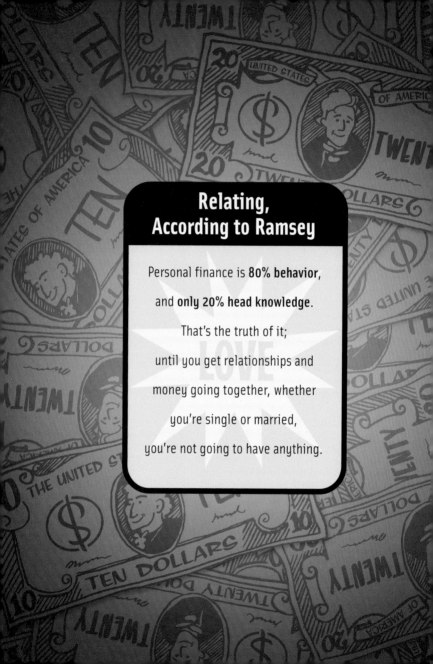

Relating, According to Ramsey

Personal finance is **80% behavior**,

and **only 20% head knowledge**.

That's the truth of it;

until you get relationships and

money going together, whether

you're single or married,

you're not going to have anything.

> **B**ut if anyone does not provide for his own,
> and especially for those of his household,
> he has denied the faith and is worse than an unbeliever.

1 TIMOTHY 5:8

Life is an exciting business, and most exciting when it is lived for others.

>HELEN KELLER

The credit belongs to the man who is actually in the arena; whose
face is marred by dust and sweat and blood; who strives valiantly;
who errs and comes short again and again; who know the great
enthusiasms, the great devotions, and spends himself in a worthy cause;
who at the best knows in the end the triumph of high achievement;
and who at worst, if he fails, at least he fails while daring greatly.

>THEODORE ROOSEVELT

> IF YOU RECORD YOUR SPENDING IN YOUR CHECK REGISTER,
> I CAN TAKE ONE LOOK AND KNOW
> A LOT ABOUT YOUR VALUE SYSTEM.
> IF I CAN LOOK AT YOUR CHECK REGISTER AND DAILY CALENDAR,
> I WILL KNOW YOU. NOT WHO YOU SAY YOU ARE—
> BUT WHO YOU REALLY ARE, DEEP DOWN INSIDE.
> *—Dave Ramsey*

Children have never been very good at listening to their elders,
but they have never failed to imitate them.

>JAMES BALDWIN

Success is more a function of common sense than it is of genius.

>AN WANG

Never get so busy making a living that you forget to make a life.

Just about the time most of us get our summer vacations paid off,
it's time to start worrying about Christmas.

Money may be the husk of many things, but not the kernel.
It brings you food, but not appetite; medicine,
but not health; acquaintances, but not friends; servants,
but not faithfulness; days of joy, but not peace and happiness.

>HENRIK IBSEN

He who tends to be "appetite rich" will become "relationship-poor."

For even when we were with you, we commanded you this:
If anyone will not work, neither shall he eat.

II THESSALONIANS 3:10

"Although we are not out of debt yet—we are on our way! We have been married for nearly sixteen years and in all that time I've always handled our finances. It was always my job to pay the bills and handle all the banking and the like. We have three children, and there have been many times I've felt such a burden on my shoulders to stretch the money to pay all the necessities, bills, and still have some left. . . . Recently my husband and I sat down together and made out a budget. This is something we had never done, much less work on it together! I'm not saying my husband didn't help me, but growing up that's how his parents handled their finances and so it carried over to our marriage. What a burden has been lifted from my shoulders just because we are doing it together.

Our children have been seeing and hearing us working on the budget, etc. So they are aware of our plans and grasping the concepts with us. [My 8-year-old] handed me her "pretend" credit card that came with her toy cash register. She still has the cash register, but said to me when she plays with it from now on—she will pay CASH! What a feeling—my husband and I have already begun changing our family tree!" —Janet

"When I became a widow, I felt like I had to give my kids a lot of "things," because they didn't have a Dad. But reality has finally hit me that a secure future is worth more than all the stuff they could ever have. I've changed my thinking and theirs, too." —Debbie

"I am a fourth grader and I am very smart. My mother listens to you and we have to listen to your show when she picks us up from school (that's how I know about you). I will share what I am doing with my classmates at my church. This is called serving my parents.**"**

— Franz

"When my husband and I first started sinking was when we decided to buy a house. One improvement led to another and soon we had a HEL loan! This was in addition to all the revolving credit that was present before the move. I would be lying to say it was easy or it is easy, but we have finished two years of credit counseling and are continuing to walk through the steps. We have $500 worth of credit to pay off, then we'll have our van and our home left. In addition, we have our $1,000 beginning savings in place and have managed to get our Life insurance coverage. This brought us together, cemented our unity so to speak, pointed us both in the same direction, uncovered and revealed our flaws for each other to see, but above all it really made us so grateful and appreciative of what God has given.**"**

— Gracie and Chris

>Chapter 4

Wheeling and Dealing

(Negotiating for Bargains)

*Dishonest scales are
an abomination to the Lord,
but a just weight
is His delight.*

PROVERBS 11:1

Win-Win Deals

Bargaining is great fun—everyone enjoys a good deal, especially if they can buy the same stuff at eighty percent (or less) of what everyone else is paying for it. There are a couple of things you need to know about bargaining, however. First, you have to tell the truth. Second, you cannot set out to harm the other party. It all seems pretty straightforward, doesn't it? But you need to examine your heart, your motivation, because you don't have to hurt someone to get a great deal; try to make it a win-win situation.

There are three basic things you need to know to be an expert bargain hunter. First, you have to learn to negotiate everything. The second helpful hint is to have patience. Third, know where to shop.

When I think about negotiating, I'm reminded of a story told by Bill Ury and Robert Fisher about two elderly ladies who are arguing over the last orange in the house. They decide that the fair thing to do is cut it in half. One lady takes the peel from her half and bakes a cake. The other takes the flesh from her half to eat. Had they negotiated properly, both could have had one hundred percent of the part of the orange that they wanted.

Don't be afraid to ask for the deal. You may be good at crafts, or you may be an accountant—be willing to trade your talent or skills. I once took one of my books, which at the time retailed for $12.95, and offered it in exchange for an $8 haircut. My barber looked a bit miffed—even though dollar-for-dollar, he was getting the better end of it—so I asked him what the problem was. He said, "well, you keep talking about me ripping you off for cutting your hair. I'm not charging you for cutting it; I'm charging you a hunting fee." That's the thanks I get, being a bald guy with a bestseller: a cheeky barber.

Remember that cash has power and so does the ability to walk away. Chances are, if you have the cash—I'm talking greenbacks here, not a check—to pay for an item, you can start negotiating a better deal than the guy who has a check, credit card, or loan application. If you can't arrive at an agreement, walk away. Without fanfare, hostility, or remorse. If you're not ready to walk away, simply say "That's not good enough," and shut up. I mean it—fall silent, right then and there. And until they come up with something that is good enough, just repeat that line with each offer. You can always walk away—and by doing so, you will develop a little patience. Good deals can happen to those who wait.

There are so many directions a person can go to find bargains—so many routes besides the one that heads toward the mall. Individuals sell things all the time—ever heard of the classifieds? Check out your local newspaper and see what I'm talking about. Public auctions—while I'll issue a *caveat emptor* right here, I will say that if you know what you're doing, and know what you're buying, you can get some great deals. I once bought a $4,000 copier for $225 at an auction. Estate sales, garage sales, yard sales—great places to find bargains, great places to practice your negotiating techniques. Flea markets—the mother ship of the American bargain. Couponing—take the time and clip away! Take advantage of refunds and rebates, buy foreclosures, scan the repo lots for cars. Pawn and consignment shops offer great deals on grown-up toys and clothing.

Here's one you might not have thought about: check your paper to see when a convention or trade show is in town—circulate through the vendor exhibits and make deals on whatever strikes your fancy. They don't want to pack the stuff up and ship it—watch a twenty-dollar bill pay for five hundred dollars' worth of cookware. The rep doesn't want to fool with the stuff—he'd much rather be rid of it.

To sum up what I'm saying here: Everything is negotiable. At some point. At some time. In some quantity. In some color. It works, folks.

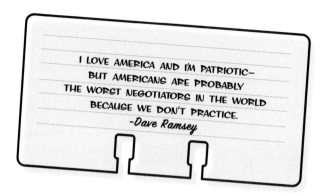

I LOVE AMERICA AND I'M PATRIOTIC—
BUT AMERICANS ARE PROBABLY
THE WORST NEGOTIATORS IN THE WORLD
BECAUSE WE DON'T PRACTICE.
—Dave Ramsey

Find something you like doing so much you'd do it for nothing.

Then learn to do it so well, they'll pay you, and you've got it made.

People with open minds must be careful these days.

There are a lot of others around intent on throwing rubbish into them.

Success is being able to hire someone to mow the lawn

while you play golf for exercise.

> **S**o they brought their livestock to Joseph, and Joseph gave them bread in exchange for the horses, the flocks, the cattle of the herds, and for the donkeys. Thus he fed them with bread in exchange for all their livestock that year.
>
> **GENESIS 47:17**

If at first you don't succeed,
go back and do it the way your wife said to in the first place.

High finance is like billiards: the object is to fill your pockets
without getting behind the eight ball.

Blessed are they who have nothing to say
and who cannot be persuaded to say it.

>JAMES RUSSELL LOWELL

7 Important Things to Know about Negotiating

1. Always tell the absolute truth.

2. Use the power of cash.

3. Understand and use "walk-away power."

4. Use the phrase "That is not good enough."

5. Shut up.

6. Good guy/Bad guy tactics, where two salespeople "play" off other.
"Good Guy" is on your side, but "Bad Guy" is hard-nosed. Be aware that they're playing a game, and your money is the prize.

7. "If I" give you this, "then" I can take away that.

Opportunities come in unexpected packages.

Cars are not the only things subject to recall by the maker.

Duct tape is like the Force.
It has a light side, a dark side, and it holds the universe together.

>CARL ZWANZIG

"How can I show my appreciation?"
said a woman client to Clarence Darrow, after he had won her legal case.
"My dear madam," said the great lawyer, "ever since the Phoenicians
invented money there has been only one answer to that question."

ou shall not steal, nor deal falsely, nor lie to one another.

LEVITICUS 19:11

> I CAN WALK INTO DEPARTMENT STORES AND START LAYING $100 BILLS DOWN AND BUY STUFF. MY WIFE GETS EMBARRASSED, BUT I JUST HAVE NO SHAME ABOUT THIS AT ALL. I'VE BEEN BROKE AND I DON'T WANT TO BE THERE AGAIN. THE FLOW OF MONEY OUT OF MY HAND INTO SOMEONE ELSE'S IS A REAL TOUCHY THING WITH ME.
> —*Dave Ramsey*

Pray for a good harvest, but continue to hoe.

We must all suffer from one of two pains:

the pain of discipline or the pain of regret.

Discipline weighs ounces—regret weighs tons.

>JIM ROHN

Happiness is not a state to arrive at, but a manner of traveling.

>MARGARET LEE RUNBECK

NEGOTIATING IS NOT ALWAYS ABOUT THE PRICE.
SOMETIMES, IT'S ABOUT OTHER THINGS OR HELPING SOMEONE.
USE THE 'IF-I' PLAN: GIVE SOMETHING, THEN TAKE SOMETHING.
"IF I... PAY YOU, HIRE YOU, TEACH YOU, SELL YOU..."
THEN MAKE CERTAIN SOMEONE IS PERFORMING A SERVICE
OR PAYING YOU MONEY IN RETURN.
—Dave Ramsey

If you want something you've never had,
you'll have to do something you've never done.

For some stingy people, the last will becomes the last won't.

I said to the boastful, "Do not deal boastfully,"
And to the wicked, "Do not lift up the horn."

PSALM 75:4

You pays your money and you takes your choice.

>PUNCH

When your ship finally does come in,
how come the IRS is on the dock unloading it?

> Behold, My Servant shall deal prudently;
He shall be exalted and extolled and be very high.

ISAIAH 52:13

A heavy purse makes a light heart.

>IRISH PROVERB

The difference between a successful person and others
is not a lack of strength, not a lack of knowledge,
but rather a lack of will.

VINCE LOMBARDI

Turning Hair Loss into Hope

Sarah Breedlove Walker was one of the first American women millionaires. Born to emancipated slaves and orphaned by age seven, she worked as a domestic and laundress until her late thirties. During the 1890s her hair began to fall out, and she experimented with various remedies until she developed a solution; technically, she was her own first customer for Madam C. J. Walker Manufacturing. Her husband knew the newspaper business and helped her market her beauty products through African-American publications.

Determined to grow the company, Walker traveled around, teaching other African-Americans how to use and market her lines. Despite a bit of criticism—particularly from those who felt that naturally curly hair should not be straightened—Walker's business continued to thrive; while she helped others gain self-respect and dignity, they in turn were helping to spread the word about honest grooming products specially designed for African-Americans. These supporters were often called "Walker agents," and many became successful entrepreneurs during a time when many African-Americans did not have many education or career opportunities.

Walker traveled beyond U. S. borders, expanding to Latin America and the Caribbean, talking to churches, organizations, and civic groups. At one time, it is estimated that she had more than three thousand Walker Agents. They met annually to exchange ideas and consider new products.

Walker lived lavishly, but gave lavishly. She managed her business carefully and prayerfully, and treated her supporters well. She did not let race, gender, or circumstances quench her hope, and she remained true to herself. Never forgetting her roots, she was an active contributor to many religious, charitable, educational, and civil rights organizations; the NAACP, for example, ultimately inherited her home in Irving-on-Hudson.

Sarah Breedlove Walker received a blessing that she used to bless others. Had she given up and accepted something like hair loss, thousands of people would have continued to struggle, including Walker herself. She offered a "win-win" deal to African-Americans during a time when most had very little opportunity to show their talent or enjoy little extras like beauty and grooming products. Walker provided tangible hope and left a legacy that encouraged others to surpass her own dreams.

Do all the good you can

By all the means you can

In all the ways you can

In all the places you can

At all the times you can

To all the people you can

As long as you ever can.

> J O H N   W E S L E Y

Ten cents used to be a lot of money. How dimes have changed.

DON'T BE MANIPULATIVE WITH THESE THINGS.
TRY TO HELP PEOPLE WHEN YOU'RE MAKING A PURCHASE.
DO BUSINESS AND DO DEALS WITH PEOPLE
WHO NEED YOUR HELP AND SELL THINGS TO PEOPLE.
-Dave Ramsey

Testimonials

"We are all helping one another to get out of debt. One of the guys just sold his brand new truck because of your show, and I have a Camaro convertible (brand new) that I will be selling. We all had our cards hanging around our necks with plastic chains. Thanks a lot!"

—Diane, Ray, Trudy, Steve

"After walking around (feeling dazed) for two days, I pulled out my budget and began working with the figures. By Thursday I got the nerve to pull out the credit cards and begin snipping. It was like cutting away my safety net.

Since that time I have pulled off a quickie yard sale, set up an interview for a part-time job, decreased my cellular phone expense and found a used bookstore where I can satisfy my book addiction (not included in budget). The reaction I've gotten has been . . . everything from embracing what I'm saying, wanting to know more, skepticism, and rejection. My new lifestyle has become an inconvenience to my "spending buddies." I guess that's part of it.

I have a long way to go to even see the light of day but it is a journey I hope I will stay on forever. This Sunday morning, with the sun shining and the warm breeze blowing against my skin, I'm happy and at peace. Thank you for showing me the way."

—Connie

Credit Card

Good Boy!

Chapter 5

Digging Out From Under
(Dumping Debt)

The rich rules over the poor,

and the borrower is servant to the lender.

PROVERBS 22:7

Quit Buying Debt

I have such a weird way of looking at things. I get a lot of criticism; I get these letters that say, "Dave, you're weird." Well, if normal is broke, then I want to be as weird as I can be.

Debt is a major product that's been marketed to us since the 1960s. We don't look at it as a product—we can go into a store and avoid a salesperson by telling them we're "just looking." But we don't do that with debt—those banks have some savvy marketing, and we're in there saying "give me one of everything you've got! Please!" Can you imagine running a shoe store and having some customer say that to you? But we do it all the time with banks—and those guys sell debt.

Now before I start getting more criticism, let me say that banks aren't evil; but banks are a business. They have profits to make, just like any other business. But folks, when you borrow money, you become a slave.

How many of you started out rich? How many of you started out wanting to look rich, so you bought a television set, stereo, speakers, and maybe a cabinet to house it all on ninety days, same-as-cash? That's how we started our lives. But the "success" of those things is short-lived; soon enough, you'll want a new car, furniture, house . . . and you're in this vicious cycle of keeping up, paying off, but then purchasing newer and better in order to keep up again. Soon enough, your keeping-up pace will exceed the paying-off pace and you'll be drowning in debt.

Larry Burkett says, "We spend the first five or ten years of our adult lives trying to achieve the same standard of living as our parents; but we forget that it took our parents thirty-five years to get there."

So how do you dump debt? I will tell you right now that it ain't easy. And it ain't quick. You'll be working hard. You'll be selling stuff. You'll be driving clunkers. Your life might not look as pretty for a while, but a healthy bank account is a beautiful thing. And beauty is pain, right?

Stop borrowing from friends; destroy that gold card, or any other plastic you're carrying in your wallet, unless it's a library card; no more home equity loans, car loans, or even those "debt CONsolidation loans" you see hawked on television, disguised as "we're going to help you" loans.

And get ready to be called weird. Welcome to the club.

Getting money is like digging with a needle;
spending it is like water soaking into sand.

>JAPANESE PROVERB

The greatest oak was once a little nut that held its ground.

Here's to our creditors.
May they be endowed with the three virtues—
hope, faith, and charity.

Owe no one anything except to love one another,

for he who loves another has fulfilled the law.

ROMANS 13:8

Is the light at the end of the tunnel an oncoming train?

Dollars and sense should go together.

I WAS DRIVING A '78 CADILLAC—WE CALLED IT THE 4-WHEEL PARACHUTE BECAUSE WHEN WIND GOT INTO THE TORN VINYL ROOF, THE COVER WOULD BILLOW OUT—AND I PULLED UP TO A STOPLIGHT WHERE A FRIEND OF MINE WAS IN THE NEXT LANE, IN HIS SHINY LEXUS. HE STARTED LAUGHING AT ME, AND I SMILED, WAVING BACK. WHAT HE DIDN'T SEE WAS MY DAY PLANNER, WHERE I WROTE: "SOON, I WILL BUY YOUR COMPANY. FOR CASH."

—*Dave Ramsey*

Weigh to Go!

Say what you want about her, there's few people who can top Sarah, Duchess of York when it comes to pluck. And she certainly needed all the pluck she could find after her divorce from Prince Andrew, because one thing she didn't have was money. That's a tough reality when you are millions of dollars in debt—and your mother-in-law has already bailed you out once.

Before her stint as a royal, Sarah Ferguson had held various positions in publishing and sales, and that was a good thing. Since her divorce, she has written columns and books, served as a spokesperson, made special appearances on television shows, appeared in commercials, and even moved back in with her ex-husband in an effort to straighten out her finances.

Now few of us will be handed lucrative opportunities like television appearances, but few of us also have the opportunity to be millions of dollars in debt; I'm talking millions of dollars in debt, folks—not thousands—and no job, no safety net. Ferguson was used to safety nets; can you imagine opening up your department store bill and discovering you owe seven figures? From a relative perspective, Ferguson capitalized on what she did best and this plan got her out of a jam. She didn't sit around and wait for her pleas to be heard—she figured out fairly quickly that the only person that would get her out of this mess was herself.

She's made mistakes, mistakes that are far more public than our own. Despite her mistakes, she continues to plug along and is very honest about her bad spending habits. Not only that, but she's endured harsh criticism from her own country. You can whine about your debt, let the creditors say things about you, but at least the general American public couldn't care less and your name isn't smeared on all the tabloids each time you buy a pair of socks.

She's had an uphill battle, most of it fighting through messes she made; but Sarah Ferguson's fighting spirit has rallied. She is, at the very least, a survivor of the debt monster attack.

Credit Card Crumbs

Consumer Reports says that we have more than **one billion pieces of plastic** with one of the major cards in **74% of all U. S. households.**

Ram Research Corporation states there are more than **43 million Discover cards, 33 million Citibank Visas, 25 million American Express, and 22 million AT&T Universal Visas.**

According to *The Wall Street Journal*, there are more than **26 million Sears cards** with **over 700,000 applications per month.**

MasterCard, Visa, American Express, and Discover will spend a combined **$567 billion** this year in advertising.

Advertising Age states that credit card companies will send consumers **1.1 billion pieces of mail** in 2002.

USA Today notes that Citibank, the largest issuer of Visa, will **spend $10 million this year** just marketing credit cards to **high school and college students.**

Colleges can earn $50,000 to $100,000 per year just to allow a credit card company to operate on campus. **Credit cards have become a rite of passage.**

The wicked borrows and does not repay,

but the righteous shows mercy and gives.

PSALMS 37:21

If you make money your god, it will plague you like the devil.

>HENRY FIELDING

It's so unfair. Opportunity only knocks once,

but my car knocks every time I drive it over forty miles an hour.

Spendthrift: someone who thinks a nest egg is for the birds.

If you had your life to live over again, you'd need more money.

>CONSTRUCTION DIGEST

If you want to write something that will live forever, sign a mortgage.

A small trouble is like a pebble.

Hold it too close to your eye

and it fills the whole world and puts everything out of focus.

Hold it at proper viewing distance

and it can be examined and properly classified.

Throw it at your feet

and it can be seen in its true setting,

just one more tiny bump on the pathway to eternity.

>CELIA LUCE

The Debt Snowball

The debt snowball looks like this: you list your debts, smallest to largest. And you've got your $1,000 in the bank first, okay? Pay minimum payments on everything but the smallest one, regardless of the interest rate. Each one you pay off, strike a line through it and take that money and dump it into the next one, in addition to the minimum payment. Keep it up until you're out of debt. It feels so good to knock out those bills!

MY DEBT CHART

Prosperity is that period between the last installment
and the next purchase.

Do not be one of those who shakes hands in a pledge,
One of those who is surety for debts;
If you have nothing with which to pay,
Why should he take away your bed from under you?

PROVERBS 22:26–27

You know something's wrong when you start moonlighting
to keep up the payments on all those labor-saving devices.

The difference between a luxury and a necessity is
directly proportional to your inability to pay for it.

Anytime someone tells you they're offering you
the opportunity of a lifetime, be careful.
It'll probably cost your life savings.

Most of us would be happy to pay as we go
if only we could catch up to where we've been.

You can't judge a book by its cover,
but you can know a lot about a corporation by its Chapter 11.

YOU HAVE $1,000, NO PERSONAL DEBT
EXCEPT MAYBE A MORTGAGE,
AND NOW YOU'RE SAVING THREE TO SIX MONTHS'
LIVING EXPENSES. WHAT WOULD YOUR LIFE BE LIKE
WITH NO PAYMENTS EXCEPT YOUR HOME
AND $10,000 IN THE BANK? FINANCIALLY PEACEFUL.
—Dave Ramsey

The fuel that keeps people moving faster
than the speed of worry is money.

>WILFRID SHEED

There are no shortcuts to any place worth going.

>BEVERLY SILLS

It's a matter of giving more to this world than you take from it,
so when you die, you don't owe it anything.

>GORDON PARKS

> Nevertheless, lest we offend them, go to the sea, cast in a hook,
> and take the fish that comes up first. And when you have
> opened its mouth, you will find a piece of money;
> take that and give it to them for Me and you.
>
> **MATTHEW 17:27**

Testimonials

"One young 'pregnant for the first time' couple came to our class because they had a dream of her being a stay-at-home Mom. They really got serious and opted out of two leased vehicles. By the end of the thirteen weeks, they had dumped $35,500 in debt! She will now be able to be a full-time Mom!

Another 'pregnant for the first time' couple that had been in our class last spring came up to us at church last week. Baby is due any day, they are out of debt and have more money left each month than they know what to do with!" —Debby

"Today I balanced our checkbook—my balance and the bank's balance were $0.01 apart. That is the closest I have ever been in twenty-six years of marriage. My husband and I actually celebrated this achievement along with the facts that we have $1,000 in an emergency fund, $25,000+ in an IRA, 401k, and our mortgage is at 7.25 % (refinanced from 10.5%). We haven't had a late notice in over a year; returned checks, none in two years; our medical bills are coming down; and the cancelled credit card will be paid in five months. Last Christmas was cash only. All the little things that used to discourage me have ceased: mailbox full of bills, late notices, no good news. We have a long way to go . . . [but] please accept this sincere thank-you." —Beverly

>Chapter 6

Maximize Your Legacy
(Making It Count)

> *The plans of the diligent*
>
> *lead surely to plenty,*
>
> *but those of everyone who is hasty,*
>
> *surely to poverty.*
>
> PROVERBS 21:5

Managing God's Money

Your money is yours . . . right? Wrong! Everything belongs to God—not just stuff you don't want, or no longer use—everything. You're allowed to manage it, and sometimes you manage a little or a lot, but keep in mind that it all belongs to Him.

Remember that scene in *The Jerk* where Steve Martin is losing everything and he says, "I'll be okay if I could just take this and have this . . ." And he's walking down the street with things hanging off of him? I get like that sometimes. The truth is, however, you can't pick and choose; it all belongs to God.

So is it bad for you to have things? No. Is it bad for you to be wealthy by the world's standards and be a full-blown Christian? No. Not at all. The Bible does not say that money is the root of all evil; it's the *love of money* that is the root of all kinds of evil (1 Timothy 6:10). What that means is that you need balance and perspective.

There are varying levels of management discussion and of management delegation, but the top one is management-level delegation—where you take a concept and it's up to you to make it happen. For example, if I'm the regional manager for Burger King, my CEO doesn't want to know how many Whoppers were flipped; he wants to know gross sales expenses and profits.

That's how God manages money. He gives you management-level delegation but doesn't tell you exactly what to do with it. He's not going to say, "don't buy that Lexus." As a general rule, however, He will say "don't build a tower without first counting the cost." So guess what? Here comes the B-word again: budget.

Now since we're asset managers for the Lord, we also need to talk about the T-word: tithe. Just to clarify, the word tithe means tenth. When people say, "I'm tithing five percent," what they're really saying is "I'm tenthing a twentyith." Some can give more than a tenth; others might have to give less for a while. Tithe should be a minimum goal, but really all I'm encouraging you to do is give. Give to your local church; give to charities; give, give, give.

On top of that, your tithe cannot come from the "what's left over" pocket; if you tithe this way, then you don't tithe. I should know, I tried doing it that way for a while. Nope, your tithe has to come first—that's right, first—before anything else is paid. God is not a waiter; you are not giving Him a tip.

"First fruits" means right off the top, and first fruits are how you should give. There are twenty-two mentions of first fruits in the Bible, and what it means to you is that when you look at your check register and see your deposit, the next entry should be your tithe check. Bills and budget come next—no exceptions. Believe me, I've tried.

There are three reasons the Lord wants us to give: first, it reminds us of His ownership; second, it is an act of praise and worship; third, for spiritual warfare. It says very clearly right around all that tithe Scripture that He will "rebuke the devourer" so you can expect Him to post angels to assist you. I truly believe that—therefore, I have big, bad, square-shouldered angels stationed right around my children and property.

Once you leave this world, what you leave behind is up to you—a legacy of properly managed money, or a curse of debt and mishandling. You see, it's not just about how you live today; it's what your children will learn and continue to do long after you're gone. And their children, and their children, and their children.

What kind of values do you want to instill? How can you be sure that when your management job is over, your children can pick up where you left off, and operate in the same way? By making the changes now in your own life, and including your family in the process.

DID YA KNOW?

... that 75% of Forbes' 400 said,
when surveyed, that the number one key
to building wealth is to be debt free.

Great souls have wills; feeble ones have only wishes.

>CHINESE PROVERB

Said one disgruntled businessman to another, "I wanted my son to have
a share in my business, but the government beat him to it."

YOU CAN SING YOUR HEART OUT AND NEVER GIVE,

AND MISS THE FULLNESS OF WORSHIP.

-Dave Ramsey

Noah was quite a financier:

he floated his stock when everyone else was being liquidated.

> **B**ehold, I send you out as sheep in the midst of wolves.
> Therefore be wise as serpents and harmless as doves.
>
> **MATTHEW 10:16**

Comedian Richard Pryor, critically burned in an accident, told Johnny
Carson that when you're seriously ill, money isn't important.
He said: "All I could think of was to call on God.
I didn't call the Bank of America once."

Happiness is like a butterfly.
The more you chase it, the more it will elude you.
But if you turn your attention to other things,
it comes and softly sits on your shoulder.

Supporting the Savior

Mary Magdalene was roughly the same age as Jesus. Most of what we know about her is from the gospels, but many have tried to give her a notoriety the likes of today's tabloids.

What we do know is that she grew up on the western bank of the Sea of Galilee and that Jesus exorcised seven demons from her body. Several women from the area followed Jesus on His travels, Mary being one of them. She was the first person to see Jesus after the Resurrection, and the first to deliver the news to the surviving disciples. Some say Mary spent the last decades of her life in southern France.

She has been accused of being a prostitute and being resented by the twelve disciples for her close relationship with Christ. There is no hard evidence to support either claim. Her place of death is the subject of dispute, also.

Many think that she might have been a hairdresser, and by calling her "Mary Magdalene," the disciples were sharing a good-natured joke or nickname of sorts. There's even a rumor that she was the true author of the fourth gospel! It's a good thing those tabloid papers didn't exist in those days; poor Mary would have been a regular in the headlines.

What is often forgotten is that Mary was a benefactor in Jesus' ministry. Mary was wealthy and served as a major contributor to Jesus' ministry before and after His crucifixion. Because of her generosity, it's quite possible that Jesus and the disciples did not have to take on as many projects to earn money and could, instead, focus on the needs of others. Mary gave to a cause and a person she believed in—but despite all of the money she gave, she could not outgive God. The Lord keeps His promises—and Mary was healed, saved, and given eternal life. Had Mary remained in Magdala after meeting Jesus, she would have been blessed; but certainly by traveling with, interacting with, and giving financial support to Jesus, she was able to receive God's full blessing.

> **F**or what is your life?
> It is even a vapor that appears for a little time
> and then vanishes away.
>
> **JAMES 4:14**

I want to live as though Jesus died for me yesterday,
rose this morning, and is coming again tomorrow.

Plan the following week by this Friday.

Wall Street is the din of inequity.

Show me someone who's spent all their inheritance

and I'll show you someone

who doesn't have the cents they were born with.

DOES GOD NEED YOUR MONEY?

IF THAT'S WHAT THIS WAS ABOUT,

THERE WOULD BE A GREASY SPOT WHERE YOU'RE SITTING

& HE'D TAKE IT. HE DOESN'T NEED YOUR COTTON-PICKING MONEY.

GOD TELLS YOU TO GIVE FOR YOU; HE KNOWS HOW YOU'RE WIRED,

HE KNOWS WHAT IT DOES FOR YOU.

-Dave Ramsey

The difference between genius and stupidity
is that genius has its limits.

Why do they call it Wall Street
when it's always going through either the ceiling or the floor?

You know you're in trouble when the strange noise from your car
is the mechanic laughing underneath it.

Give portions to seven, yes to eight,
for you do not know what disaster may come upon the land.

ECCLESIASTES 11:2, NIV

Legacy Lesson

With careful planning, you could not only relieve your own debt, but set your children up for a debt-free start as well. Use the debt snowball to recover from your own debt, and carefully save and invest according to the seven baby steps listed at the beginning of this book. You could actually buy a house for your children and in turn, have them put their mortgage "payment" in a solid mutual fund. When your grandchildren are ready for their first home, your children will be ready to continue the tradition you started!

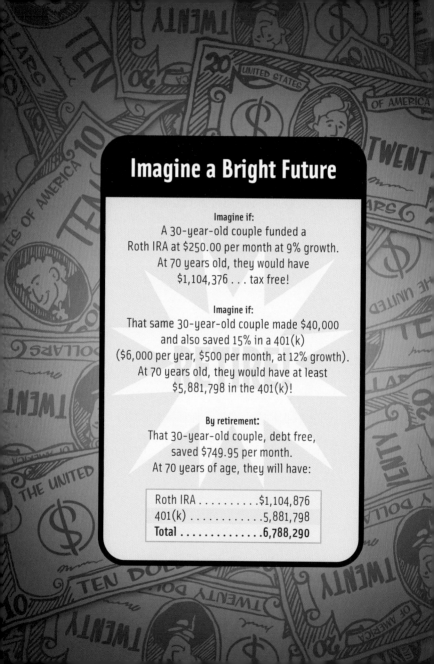

Imagine a Bright Future

Imagine if:
A 30-year-old couple funded a
Roth IRA at $250.00 per month at 9% growth.
At 70 years old, they would have
$1,104,376 . . . tax free!

Imagine if:
That same 30-year-old couple made $40,000
and also saved 15% in a 401(k)
($6,000 per year, $500 per month, at 12% growth).
At 70 years old, they would have at least
$5,881,798 in the 401(k)!

By retirement:
That 30-year-old couple, debt free,
saved $749.95 per month.
At 70 years of age, they will have:

Roth IRA	$1,104,876
401(k)	5,881,798
Total	6,788,290

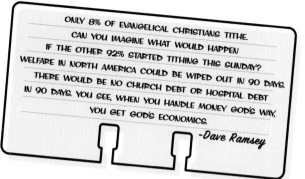

ONLY 8% OF EVANGELICAL CHRISTIANS TITHE. CAN YOU IMAGINE WHAT WOULD HAPPEN IF THE OTHER 92% STARTED TITHING THIS SUNDAY? WELFARE IN NORTH AMERICA COULD BE WIPED OUT IN 90 DAYS. THERE WOULD BE NO CHURCH DEBT OR HOSPITAL DEBT IN 90 DAYS. YOU SEE, WHEN YOU HANDLE MONEY GOD'S WAY, YOU GET GOD'S ECONOMICS.

—Dave Ramsey

No one would have remembered the Good Samaritan
if he only had good intentions. He had money as well.

>MARGARET THATCHER

Wall Street is very hygienic.
There, you either clean up or end up taking a bath.

Riches are not forbidden, but the pride of them is.

>ST. JOHN CHRYSOSTOM

Just as riches are an impediment to virtue in the wicked,

so in the good they are an aid of virtue.

>ST. AMBROSE

He who trusts in his riches will fall.

PROVERBS 11:28

Consider the postage stamp:

its usefulness consists in the ability

to stick to one thing till it gets there.

>JOSH BILLINGS

Yesterday is history

Tomorrow's a mystery

Today is a gift

That's why it's called the Present.

Testimonials

"You certainly brought out the relativity of the Scriptures concerning tithing and finances. Your perspective on this subject and the sincerity of your words confirms that your message is an anointed one.**"**
—Venerria

"Bringing my financial life in line with Scriptural principles about handling money has improved both my financial life and my spiritual life. Watching my financial situation improve through wise, Biblically sound principles has reassured me that by applying God's word and common sense, other areas of my life will improve as well. And because my financial situation is improving, I will be able to give more monetary support to my church and other worthy causes.**"**
—Jeff

Dave's Story

Basically, I grew up lower middle class like most people in Antioch, Tennessee. Mama and Daddy were working people so when I came home at twelve years old and wanted money to buy a Snickers bar at Kwik Sak, Dad said, you don't need money; you need a job. We went and printed up five hundred business cards that said "Dave's Lawns." We came back and knocked on the closest fifty doors, and Dad said, "Don't go to the door and ask these people, 'you don't want me to cut your yard, do you?'" Instead, he said, "Go in there and enthusiastically ask them for the opportunity to provide for their lawn care needs." It worked; sadly enough, I ended up at twelve years old with twenty-seven lawns to cut—nineteen of them right in a row. Right then and there I started work, W-O-R-K, a surefire money-making scheme.

Mom and Dad were in the real estate business, so we were required to attend (much to our chagrin) all the positive-thinking and sales conferences. Zig Ziglar, Tom Hopkins, Paul Harvey, and Earl Nightingale were my best buds—by the time I was sixteen, I'd been through Dale Carnegie and all these other people. At the time, I didn't think it was a lot of fun, but it certainly has shaped my life.

We were told to set goals, grasp a vision, make a plan, because at eighteen, you're outta here. When I turned eighteen, I sat for and passed my real estate licensing exam and had plans to become a real estate tycoon.

You can't be a tycoon showing houses. I learned very quickly that I needed to go into commercial real estate and that it probably would help if I had some sort of academic degree. I went to the University of Tennessee in Knoxville, worked forty to sixty hours each week selling residential real estate, carried a full load, and graduated in four years.

I have always sold, I've always worked, I've always set goals and hit them—or got close enough to them to know where I stood.

When we got married, Sharon and I started with nothing. All those things worked out like they're supposed to with the Great American Dream: academics, hard work, entrepreneurial spirit, positive thinking, goal setting . . . they all came together, and over the next several years, I got rich (at least by a kid from Antioch, Tennessee's standards). By the time I was twenty-six years old, I'd amassed about four million dollars' worth of real estate, a little over one million net worth, and about $250,000 annual income—yes, that's right, $20,000 a month in taxable cash. It was fun; it was a blast.

Sometimes you hear people say, "oh those rich people are miserable." No, they're not. It was fun; I wanted a Jaguar, so I went and got one. My wife, Sharon the princess, likes those sparkly things on her hands, so we went and got her some more because the ones she already had weren't big enough. We went to Hawaii, we liked it, so we went back. We wanted a house, we got one; it wasn't big enough, so we got another one. We got a boat, it wasn't fast enough, we got another one. You know the story—yours might not have as many zeroes on the end, but we've all kind of got a similar story from the kind of culture in which we live today. Truth then came home to roost.

Ninety-eight percent truth is a lie. Something either is the truth or, by its very definition, it is not. You can't have your truth and I'll have mine; there is a truth independent of you—the axis of the world does not run through the top of your head.

Proverbs 22:7 says the borrower is slave to the lender and for the next two and a half years, I found out about that. Our largest lender—Bank—got sold to another Bank. Probably never happens in your city, right? So when the new set of bosses noticed a 26-year-old who owed them a million-two in real estate, they freaked out. And even though I wasn't late, they called our note. We had ninety days to come up with $1.2 million. I'm the idiot who signed up for the trip; it wasn't their fault. They panicked, they were dumb, but I'm the one who signed documents that allowed them the right to ruin our life.

Our second largest lender got wind that Dave was in trouble and they called another $800,000 sixty days later. We had less than six months to come up with two million dollars, and it was all in real estate. That started a crash that lasted two-and-a-half years and caused us to lose everything we owned. We were sued so many times that we were on a first name basis with the guy at the sheriff's department; Sharon used to make him cookies.

We were foreclosed on, and finally—with a brand new baby and toddler—we were bankrupt.

After fighting it—with one hundred-hour weeks—for two-and-a-half years, I found out it doesn't matter how hard you work or how positive you think, when you do stupid things they will catch up and tackle you. There is a truth that is independent of your perception and ability to think positively. And the borrower is slave to the lender.

At the bottom of that mess, we had to make some decisions about life. Our first one was, we don't take financial advice from broke people. I got to thinking about it; who was it who told me to borrow money? My broke financial professor. What's wrong with this picture? A broke financial professor is like a shop teacher with missing fingers. So we started over, and started by talking to people who had money.

I found out if you do rich people stuff, you get to be rich people. You do poor people stuff, you get to be poor people. If you're rich people and you do poor people stuff, you become poor people. If you're poor people and you do rich people stuff you become, over time, rich people. Personal finance is eighty percent behavior and only twenty percent head knowledge. I don't care how much book knowledge you have; it's what you do that changes your life.

We spent the next fifteen years slowly, gradually living on less than we made and rebuilding our wealth. Sharon and I know this is our calling, summoned by the Lord, to share our story and plans with others who have been deceived by worldly trappings. It's not a question of what I can buy; back then and right now, I can buy just about anything.

But my heart, my motives, my peace—those cannot be bought, and therein lies the difference. God gave me a gift, and now that I recognize this and am using it for Him and His kingdom—blessings have been given in the most unexpected ways.

I'm just so glad I didn't settle for that four million dollars all those years ago. And I'm glad He didn't let me settle for it—when you ask for His best, He delivers.

Conclusion

Martin Luther King Jr. said you've got to stand for something or you'll fall for anything. Well, you've gotten an idea of where I've stood, what I've done, and where I'm headed. How about you? Have you made any decisions? It's time.

Think through this thing called life. Is it real? What is the right way to live? Is this Jesus stuff real? Just like Sharon and I had to do, it's time you started making your own list of No Matter Whats—the values by which you are going to live your life from this point forward. No Matter What . . . you fill in the blank. You've got to have some No Matter Whats; without them, you'll just crash. You've got to have some guiding values that are based on truth; not based on your feelings, your grandmother's opinion, or your brother-in-law who's broke and thinks he knows something about money.

These No Matter Whats come in handy in dealing with other life situations, too. I tell our teenage daughters that they've got to have some No Matter Whats, especially where boys are concerned. They tell me, "But Daddy, he's got a Bible!" I tell them, "Honey, I'd have carried a Bible, too, if I thought it'd work."

You've got to have some No Matter Whats. They help you gauge your progress; they give you a way out of the mess; they give clarity to your story.

For those of you who feel strapped by debt, face the music—you've played someone else's tune long enough. It will not be easy; it will not happen overnight. But until you eliminate—not pay down, not weaken, not forget about—but eliminate your debt, wealth will always be just out of reach. As long as you remain a slave, freedom remains an elusive "what-if." Trade in your What-ifs for a bunch of No Matter Whats. And watch what happens.

I know your partner isn't cooperative. I know the kids are growing overnight. I know deep down, you're not a bad person and you never intended for this to happen—but something always came up. I know the creditors are calling, the light bill needs paying, and the car is sputtering. Wolves are growling just outside your door—I know their sound, I know their ways. They were once outside my door, too.

If you're thinking, "well, that's fine for those people, but I have no debt, so this doesn't apply to me," you are the most vulnerable of all. Those wolves are hungry for you—you're like a delicacy to them—especially if you are a student or just starting out. You need to equip yourself to protect your freedom—and I hope this book has provided the first step toward doing so.

Folks, I'm living proof that despite the wolves' best efforts, a person can survive their attacks. And because I survived, generations of my family will be secure. And not only will my own family be secure, other people and organizations will receive part of the blessing, too.

That's the real reason to clean up this mess—the fun, the joy, the indescribable buoyancy of serving the Lord in a tangible way.

You can do this.
He is in your corner, and so am I.
Go forth, and God bless.

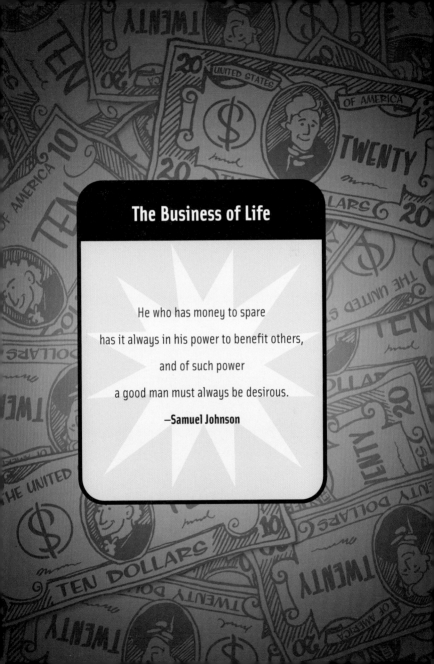

The Business of Life

He who has money to spare

has it always in his power to benefit others,

and of such power

a good man must always be desirous.

—Samuel Johnson

>Chapter 8
Your Story
(Applying Dave's Lessons)

Now that you've read this book, it's time to get real and start applying these concepts to your life. The following pages have places where you can answer basic financial questions and get some personal perspective on how your own money comes and goes.

Remember, personal finance is 80% behavior and 20% head knowledge. All I can do is get you started on the road to weirdness—the rest is up to you.

Seven Baby Steps to Financial Peace

I introduced you to these baby steps on page 15 of this book. Here you can track how you're doing.

EXAMPLES

Step	Action	Circle One		
2.	Pay off all debt with the "debt snowball."	Done / (In Progress) / Plan to Start ( )		
6.	Pay off my home early.	Done / In Progress / (Plan to Start) (4/'05)		

1.	Sock away $1,000 in an emergency fund.	Done / In Progress / Plan to Start ( )		
2.	Pay off all debt with the "debt snowball."	Done / In Progress / Plan to Start ( )		
3.	Beef up the emergency fund.	Done / In Progress / Plan to Start ( )		
4.	Invest 15% of household income into Roth IRAs and pre-tax retirement plans.	Done / In Progress / Plan to Start ( )		
5.	Save for my children's college fund.	Done / In Progress / Plan to Start ( )		
6.	Pay off my home early.	Done / In Progress / Plan to Start ( )		
7.	Build wealth through wise investments.	Done / In Progress / Plan to Start ( )		

Keeping Your Cash (Saving)

Do you have a $1,000 emergency fund?   Yes / No

Do you have any money at all saved?   Yes / No   How much? _____

Do you specifically set aside a certain amount of money each month?   Yes / No
    How much? _____

Do you have good saving habits?   Yes / No
Describe them._____

_____

What keeps you from saving more?

_____

_____

What are you going to do about it?

_____

_____

How to Eat an Elephant (Cash Flow Planning)

You absolutely must control your cash flow if you want to pay off the past, manage the present, and prepare for the future. This means making a written budget . . . every month.

When was the last time you balanced your checkbook? _____

Do you balance your checkbook regularly?   Yes / No
    How often? _____

Do you compare your checkbook with the bank statement?   Yes / No

Do you pay with plastic (debit or credit)?   Yes / No   If so, start leaving
    you cards at home or cut them up—plastic makes it too easy to overspend.

On page 44 of this book there's a simple outline of how to budget. Have you
    filled that chart in?   Yes / No

Do you have a written budget that accounts for every foreseeable expense
    for this month?   Yes / No

Do you have a written budget that accounts for every foreseeable expense
    for next month?   Yes / No

Do you have a regular "appointment" with yourself to make the next month's
    budget?   Yes / No   When?_____

Is your budget working?   Yes / No

What are you going to do to improve it?

_____

_____

Relating with Money (Finance and the Family)

Who else is affected by the way you handle money? _____
_____

Do you make yourself accountable to anyone else in the way you
    handle money?   Yes / No   Who? _____

Whose financial opinions do you trust? _____
    Why? _____

Do you and your spouse have specific financial responsibilities? (Who pays
    bills? Who makes budgets? Who balances the checkbook?)   Yes / No

Do financial issues ever affect your relationships?   Yes / No

Have you borrowed money from family or friends? _____
_____

When will you pay them back? _____

What financial habits are you teaching your children?
_____

What habits do you hope your children don't pick up?
_____

Are you making a living, making a life, or doing both?
_____

Wheeling and Dealing (Negotiating for Bargains)

Do you like good deals?   Yes / No

Do you like negotiating?   Yes / No

What's the best deal you've ever gotten? Why? _____

_____

_____

_____

Was it a win-win deal for you and the seller?   Yes / No

What's the worst deal you've ever gotten? Why? _____

_____

_____

_____

Do you consider yourself a good negotiator?   Yes / No

Do you clip coupons?   Yes / No   Scope the pawn or consignment stores?
Yes / No   Buy on sale?   Yes / No   Shop at auctions?   Yes / No

When negotiating, are you manipulative or are you going for the win-win
    deal? _____

Digging Out From Under (Dumping Debt)

Are you in debt?   Yes / No
(check ones that apply)

☐ Car?   ☐ Mortgage?
☐ School Loans?   ☐ Credit Cards?
☐ Medical Bills?   ☐ Retail Store Cards?
☐ Home Equity Loans?   ☐ Overdue Bills?
☐ Others?_____

Are you in crisis mode yet?   Yes / No

Would you like to be out of debt?   Yes / No

Are you willing to make sacrifices to get out of debt?   Yes / No

Would you sacrifice some pride?   Yes / No

Have you cut up your credit cards?   Yes / No

Do you have a written budget?   Yes / No

There are 168 hours in a week. How many hours a week do you work
for pay? _____ How many more hours could you reasonably work?

_____

What possessions are you willing to sell to pay off debt? _____

_____

What services are you willing to give up to pay off debt? _____

_____

The Debt Snowball

List all your debts from smallest to largest. Make minimum payments on all but the smallest, regardless of interest rate. Pay off the smallest as soon as possible and move on to the next one until you're out of debt.

Debt Amount	Debtor	Minimum Payment	Date Paid Off
$300	BIG RETAILER	$25	MAY 9, 2002
$6,789	CARD	$150	SEPT. 10, 2002
$14,000	AUTO STORE	$310	

EXAMPLES

You can do it!

Maximize Your Legacy (Making It Count)

Have you started planning your retirement?   Yes / No

Do you have a Roth IRA?   Yes / No

Are you investing at the maximum levels?   Yes / No / Don't know

Do you have a 401(k) or similar plan through your employer?   Yes / No

Are you investing at the maximum levels?   Yes / No / Don't know

Have you invested in solid mutual funds or other reliable options?   Yes / No

Do you have a legal will?   Yes / No

Do you have life insurance?   Yes / No

Will you be able to help your children go to college?   Yes / No

Will you be able to help your children get started in their adult lives?   Yes / No

Would you like to leave your children:

    Debts to pay off?   Yes / No

    A tidy estate?   Yes / No

    A sizeable fortune?   Yes / No

Giving God the 'First Fruits'

Have you ever made a charitable contribution?   Yes / No

Do you regularly donate money?   Yes / No

About what percentage of your income do you give away? _____ %

Is your family learning generosity from you?   Yes / No

Do you see giving as a way of worshiping the One who gave you financial resources in the first place?   Yes / No

Do you see how your spiritual life is enhanced by sharing your financial blessings?   Yes / No

Do you give God a tip from what's left over, or do you thank Him as soon as you get paid?   First fruits / Leftovers

The Bird's-Eye View

I have _____ in debt.

At my current rate, I'll be out of debt
     today / next month / next year / next decade / before retiring / never

I have _____ money in savings.

I have _____ money in investments.

I want to retire at age _____.

At my current rate, I will retire
     rich / comfortable / barely scraping by / poor / I'll never retire.

I need to change my financial behavior
     not at all / some / a lot / drastically / completely.

I will take responsibility for my financial situation: yes / no

I believe I can make the necessary changes to accomplish healthy financial
     goals for my family: yes / no

**If you answered YES to the last two questions, you're well on your way to
financial peace. You can do it. God bless.**

Want to Know More?